INTRODUCTION TO EVENT MANAGEMENT

SUNIL R HEGDE

Made with ♥ on the Notion Press Platform
www.notionpress.com

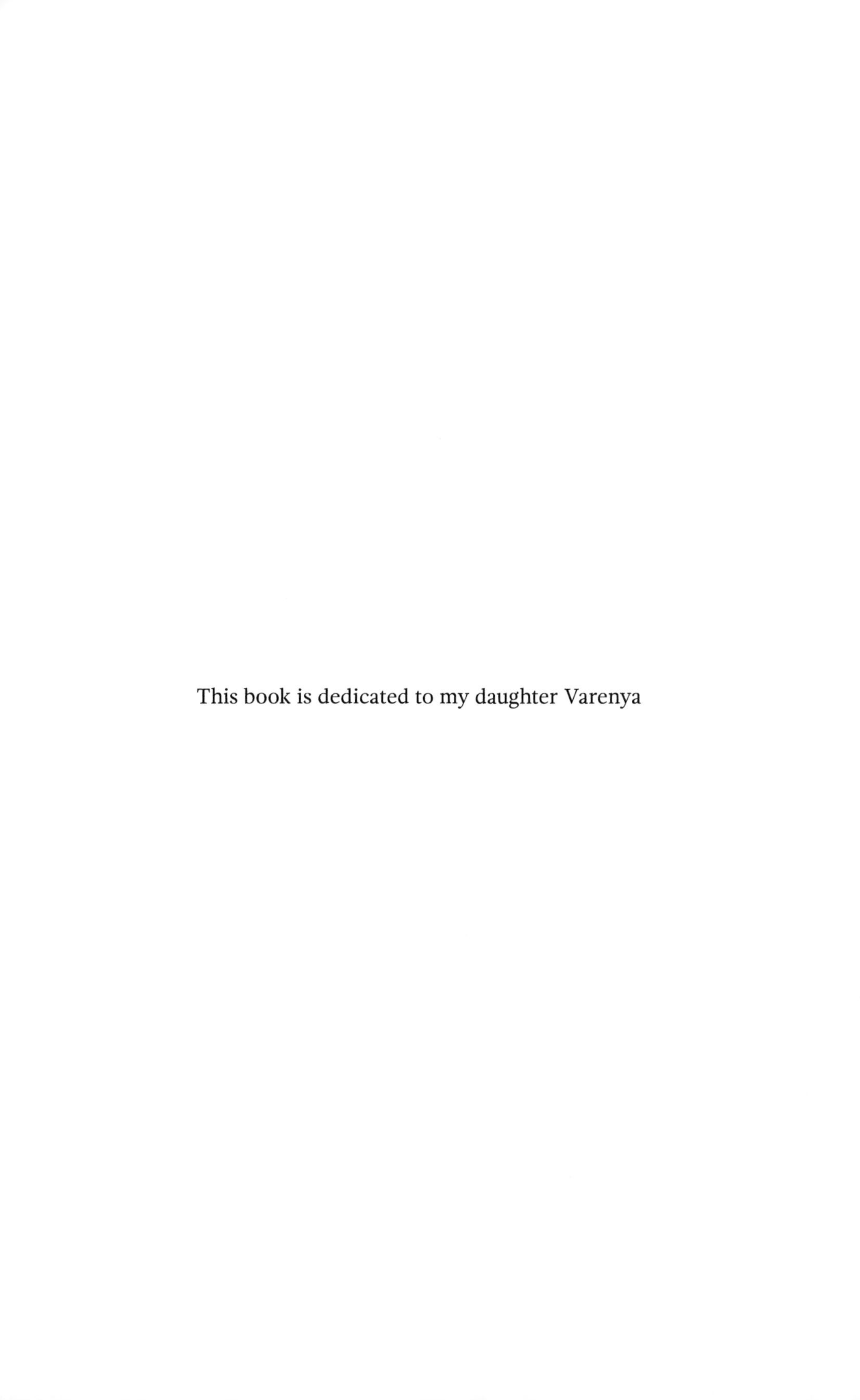

This book is dedicated to my daughter Varenya

Contents

Acknowledgements

First and foremost, praises and thanks to god, the almighty for his showers of blessings throughout the course of writing this book successfully.

I would like to thank the President-Jain University -Dr. Chenraj Roychand, who has been a guiding light in every step of my life. His words of wisdom have inspired me to write this book. I am also grateful to Dr. Dinesh Nilkant, Director –of JU-CMS for constantly supporting and encouraging me.

I also take this opportunity to thank Prof Sunitha B.K, HOD-JU-CMS, for constantly supporting me in this journey.

I should not forget to thank My wife Vidya for the encouragement and support that she provided during the course of writing this book.

I am particularly grateful to my father Mr. Raghupati Hegde, for continues inspiration and support during the preparation of the book. I must take this opportunity to thank my loving mother Mrs Sakhubai Hegde, who has been the guiding force in my life. Finally, I am sincerely obliged to all those who have directly or indirectly helped me in the completion of this book.

Sunil R Hegde

CHAPTER ONE

INTRODUCTION TO EVENT MANAGEMENT

Introduction

Events create opportunities for people to connect with an area, spend time together, celebrate and experience the diversity of cultures and foster creativity and innovation. They allow a community to come alive and provide an opportunity for a destination to showcase its tourism experience and increase economic activity. Events contribute significantly to community building, lifestyle and leisure enhancement, cultural development, tourism promotion, increased visitation, volunteer participation, fundraising, and economic development. Most importantly, events create a sense of fun and vibrancy, resulting in a strong sense of community connectivity, pride, and a sense of place.

CLASSIFICATION OF EVENTS

There are different criteria for the classification of events. The basic one classifies events as planned and unplanned. Planned events are the subject of study of event management and they require setup, management, executives, and a certain length of time. Unplanned events are accidents, natural disasters, and other similar, and they will not be taken into consideration in this unit.

1. MEGA EVENTS: Events with international appeal and truly global reach typically fall into the categories of major or mega-events. Such events have the potential to act as catalysts for local development and to deliver a range of economic, socio-cultural, environmental, and other benefits associated with image, branding, and expansion of the visitor economy, just to name a

few.

Mega-events, as the largest and highest profile of all events, invariably, require the most significant and sophisticated infrastructure development, are typically the most expensive to host, and given the competitive bidding process for such events, typically take the longest time from inception to delivery. They also tend to have the longest legacy period. However, there are also very limited opportunities for cities and countries to host these very largest events. Problems of infrastructure, facilities, transport, and cross-cultural issues are some of the limitations in the organization of these events. Despite this, many countries continue to view the investment of resources necessary to bid for and potentially host these mega-events, as one that can provide commensurate returns.

2. HALLMARK EVENT: These are the events with the distinctive quality of the program. Hallmark events are so identified with the spirit and soul of a host community that they become synonymous with the name of the place and gain widespread recognition and awareness. Hallmark events are of special importance and attractiveness both for participants and visitors, they attract the great attention of the public, contribute to the image of the destination and maintain and revitalize the tradition. Classic examples of hallmark events are Carnival in Goa, Dussehra of Kullu, and Khuajoroho Dance festival. These events are identified with the very essence of these places and their citizens and bring huge tourist revenue as well as a strong sense of local pride and international recognition.

3. MAJOR EVENTS: A major event is a large-scale event, with strong public interest and media coverage. Major events attract large numbers of visitors and help the organizers achieve good economic results. In the practice of management of events, these events are often sports-oriented, with an international reputation, and defined structure of competition for example- Formula One Grand Prix or trade fair exhibitions held at Pragati Maiden New Delhi.

4. LOCAL EVENTS: A local event is an event that is targeted mainly at local audiences and staged primarily for their social, fun, and entertainment value. These events often produce a range of benefits, including engendering pride in the community, strengthening a feeling of belonging, and creating a sense of place. They can also help with exposing people to

new ideas and experiences, encouraging participation in sports and arts activities, and encouraging tolerance and diversity. Various local events are celebrated in India such as Lohri, Baisakhi, and exhibitions to display new products

Types of Events

Events that drive international tourism in large numbers can be grouped into four main categories: Niche Events – often with close links to the host destination, whether the connection is literary, culinary, adventure sports, music festivals, etc. (e.g. Agra music festival). This category may also include events at the smaller end of the spectrum, such as the Hemis Festival of Ladakh. Such events are relatively inexpensive to organize and are likely to attract a higher proportion of high-spending international attendees.

Participatory Sports Events – for example, the world masters games, world police, and fire games, ironman events, and junior sports events. These are _destination‘ events that attract thousands of competitors from outside the host country, most of whom bring multiple people with them (spouses, friends, family) and often extend their event-related stay into a holiday.

Signature Cultural Events – events which gain an international reputation as _must see and include, for example, South by South West (SXSW) in Austin, Texas, Sonar festival in Barcelona, White Nights in Melbourne, or the Edinburgh Fringe Festival and Hogmanay, in Scotland

International Sports Events – for example, single or multi-sport events such as the World Cup Rugby, the Tour de France, and the World Championships for a variety of sports (athletics, swimming, gymnastics, etc.). Such events can not only bring in large numbers of participants and spectators but also achieve large worldwide television coverage and can play a significant role in raising the profile of the destination and the brand of the country. The biggest events of this type would be the Summer Olympic Games and the Football World Cup; however, smaller international sports events can have a similar effect on a smaller scale, often with less financial risk

BENEFITS OF EVENTS

The potential benefits of hosting major events from the perspective of the visitor economy include:

1. Structural expansion of the visitor economy: Visitors coming to a city or region for an event will contribute to a more buoyant economy, with visitor expenditure having a multiplier effect on incomes throughout related supply chains. With the multiplier effect, the host destination shall benefit in terms of employment, income, and better standards of living.
2. Alignment of tourism with other strategies: The requirements of hosting a major event can be used to, promote an integrated whole-of-government approach, and maximize synergies between relevant development and growth infrastructures constructed for events are one of the most visible lasting legacies for a host city or region and can have real impacts for tourism growth.
3. Marketing and promotion: Pre-event branding associated with the successful hosting of a major event, can provide lasting recognition of destination branding in key tourism markets, encourage return visitation of attendees or participants, and a better understanding of the focus of the event such as sport, arts, and culture, food and wine, etc.
4. Environmental impacts: The international focus often associated with major events can help to prioritize work on an often under-developed or neglected built environment and therefore the attractiveness and competitiveness of destinations. In addition, ensuring that events are managed in an environmentally friendly manner is also becoming a high priority in terms of branding

OBJECTIVES OF EVENT MANAGEMENT

Every event must have a clearly stated overall aim; otherwise, the event should not happen. Events demand a lot of concentrated effort and commitment. This commitment can only come out of a genuine belief among all participants that the aims are worthwhile and that they will be beneficial in the long term.

As well as an overall purpose any specific event must have its own set of objectives, these must be clear and set down in a way that will allow you to judge the success of the event after completion.

Objectives should always be SMART. (SPECIFIC, MEASURABLE, AGREED, REALISTIC, TIMED)

FUNCTIONS OF EVENT MANAGEMENT

1. Planning: Planning tries to optimize resource utilization across the board. A cross-functional team is a necessity here given the complexity of decision-making involved and the requirement for various event activities.

Beginning with understanding the client profile, the brief for the event, the target audience, and the number expected, a major component of any event that follows is the preparation of the event budget preparation. The planning function is involved in micro-level events coordination activities such as liaison with the creative team discussing, facilitating, and arranging for the technical specification viz., sound, light, stages, and sets. Short-listing artists and standing by artists in tune with the dictates of the creative artists is one of the most challenging tasks in the planning function. It also involves checking out alternative arrangements for locating the event, the venue, and the conditions for the event and gathering information to assist in taking a decision on whether the event would be held indoors or outdoors. While at the last task, understanding the requirements of licenses, clearances, etc., and arranging for the same as and when required is a fundamentally responsible task that the event coordinator is burdened with.

2. Organizing: These events typically have a team-based work environment and a project type of organization structure and those responsibilities are assigned to the relevant staff members in the team for the event. Coordination of the arrangements required is divided among the team members. Understanding organizing in the context of event management essentially involves the description of the activities required for an event, identifying individual and team tasks, and distributing responsibilities to coordinators. The process also involves a clear delineation of authorities and delegation of authority. Such an exercise helps in creating an intentional structure for clarity of roles and positions. These structures change with almost every event depending upon the resources available. Project-based structures are more popular in event management. Event coordinators are essentially required for the organizing part of an event. Starting from contacting the artist or performers and in case of absence or dropouts, making standby arrangements is one of the most important functions of the event coordinator. After planning and creative functions have worked out the game plan, the event coordinator then goes about fixing the date, terms, and conditions with the artist. This is followed by arranging and creating the necessary infrastructure. Planning and coordinating with the professionals for the physical availability of the sound, lights, stage, sets, and seating is followed by arranging for some softer aspects of organizing.

3. Staffing: Functional responsibilities in a project-type organization

structure define event management staffing requirements. The importance of team structure, experience, background, and expertise of team members plays a crucial role in event management. It is the size and the resource availability in the events enterprise that to an extent defines the exact role of the staff members. In the management of events manpower with various expertise is required to manage diversified activities. In a big firm, there is more scope for specialized functional personnel with limited functional responsibilities, whereas, in a small firm, there is a fusion of roles depending purely ort the availability of time and staff

Thus, while recruiting for events, one tends to feel that candidates with a past background in the hospitality industry, sales, and advertising would be ideally suited to tackle the stress and uncertain situations during the entire process Events as mentioned earlier are very physical in nature. A host of skilled and unskilled volunteers and labor staff need to be guided effectively. Functionally, one can segregate the following functional-level responsibilities that need to be addressed within the team for a specific event as discussed above in the section on organizing.

4. Leading and Coordination: The sum and substance of events as a whole revolve around interpersonal skills. The need for achieving synergy among individual efforts so that the team goal is reached is the main aim of coordination. The overall coordinators need to be managers with fantastic people skills. They are continually required to motivate the staff and other junior coordinators to work really hard given the physical nature of the job, the time constraints involved, and the one-off nature of the event.
The overall coordinator also should be able to guide the marketing and project managers and this may even mean that the experience and expertise of past events need to be passed on to relative newcomers given the shortage of professional event managers.

5. Controlling: Evaluation and correction of deviations in the event plans to ensure conformity with original plans is the gist of controlling. Evaluation is an activity that seeks to understand and measure the extent to which an event has succeeded in achieving its purpose. The purpose of an event will differ with respect to the category and variation of the event. There can be two approaches with which evaluation can be put in its proper perspective. The concept of evaluation stated above was a critical examination of digging out what went wrong. A more constructive focus for evaluation is to make

recommendations about how an event might be improved to achieve its aims more effectively.

Event management industry in India

The events industry is creative and regularly innovating. It is adapting continuously to new technology and has the potential to survive adverse economic and political circumstances as seen over the last 18 months or so. Creative content and constant innovation have played a key role in enhancing the growth of the industry and have been crucial in keeping things afloat during even the most distressing times of the pandemic.

Transitioning to the online, virtual space of event management was made possible because of the flexibility and dynamic nature of an industry such as the event and entertainment industry. This only goes to show that its deep-rooted resilience and never-give-up attitude are what define the success of the industry.

Contribution of various segments to the total revenue of the events industry

1. Digital Events are the most popular and are earning heavy revenue for organizers today. These are expected to contribute 8% of the total industry revenue.
2. The Managed Events segment has the potential to generate 53% of the total revenue in the coming 4 to 5 years.
3. Activations have the second highest potential at 22%.
4. Intellectual Property events account for only 2% of the total number of events. They contribute 17% of the industry's total revenue.
5. 75% of clients of event firms are corporates. Among these 36% are Indian companies and 19% are The Government and Public Sector contributes 11% of the total business. High Net Worth individuals contribute 9% and associations constitute the remaining 5% of clients.

Latest trends in Event Management

1. A Hybrid model of event management that is the perfect combination of the benefits of the virtual space along with the accessibility and familiarity of on-ground events is something that the industry has shifted towards since the onset of the Coronavirus pandemic. The latest technology makes it easily available and affordable for the masses, along with the numerous other benefits that an event management model of this nature will constitute.
2. AI has a role to play from the time of conceptualization of events till the

organizers collect feedback.
3. Crowdsourcing is a norm today.
4. Old is no longer gold, and so creativity, innovation, and skilling are where the future of the event looks most promising.
5. Venues are no longer stadiums and convention centers but have opened up a whole new world on virtual platforms. Various applications, tools, and websites offer a range of features, making it easily accessible, navigable, cost and time efficient, and convenient for both the event organizers as well as the customers.
6. Real-time data is being used for deciding the shape and course of events.
7. Event security is one of the priorities of organizers.
In the past decade, the number of Event Management Companies and hence the opportunities for professionals at different career levels has exponentially multiplied. Some of the best Event Management Companies in India are DNA Entertainment Networks Private Ltd, Wizcraft, Scorpio Events Management Pvt Ltd, and Cox and Kings.

The Five C'S of Event Management
1. Conceptualization: This is the first step in event planning. It refers to the main idea of the event. In this phase of event management, there are five important questions one should ask

Why the event taking place is (is there something, in particular, you want the audience to get acquainted with)?
Who are the people involved in this event?
When is the event taking place?
Where is the event happening?
What exactly is the event all about?
2. Cost: Costing is the preparation of the budget for the event, keeping in mind the cost limit set by the clients. It is necessary to know the fund available and the estimated expenses for the event. The budget must include detailed information and cost of each component of the event.
3. Canvassing: It is important to inform the guests ahead of time about the event so they can make out time from their busy schedule to participate in the event. Canvassing in event management also usually involves obtaining sponsorships, raising funds and advertising.
4. Customizing: In customization, great attention is given to the client's request to deliver an event that matches their requirements. This phase focuses on tastes of clients, client satisfaction and making the necessary

changes in the event as per the requirements of the client.

5. Carrying out: This phase involves the execution of the entire plan. It brings all planning into action. The plan is revised and evaluated with respect to client requirements, budget limit and external conditions before the plan is executed.

CHAPTER TWO

Event Planning

Event management is the process by which an event is planned, prepared, and produced. As with any other form of management, it encompasses the acquisition, allocation, direction, and control of resources to achieve one or more objectives. An event manager's job is to oversee and arrange every aspect of an event, including researching, planning, organizing, implementing, controlling, and evaluating.

Event Planning is a process of creating, communicating, and implementing a more operational roadmap to guide the actions, policies, and decision-making. It should align with the strategic plan and assist in its implementation.

Benefits of Event Planning

? To define and practically apply good event planning and financial management practices in annual planning and day-to-day work.

? To provide logic and justification for prioritizing different tasks and decisions over others.

? To systematically define tasks, logic, roles and responsibilities, strategic alignments (internally and externally), timetables, and budgets. .

? To provide an opportunity for key players such as boards, staff, stakeholders, and partners to be consulted when setting key objectives and methods.

? To provide frameworks for developing strategies related to manpower management, marketing, competitor analysis, and stakeholders.

Event Planning Steps

1. Research and Goal Setting

Depending on the type of event you are planning, you may need to conduct

some research before you get started. Some event planning companies will skip this crucial step and it can mean disaster for the success of the event.
During the research process you should interview the person or team that is responsible for hosting the event. Find out exactly what their goals are – raising money, training, networking with other professionals, sharing new ideas, etc.
Have a list of questions prepared for the research phase in order to maximize efficiency. You'll need to know the budget for the event, the date, and about how many people are expected to attend.
After you have completed your research you can document the goals and objectives of the event. Your goals and objectives should be clear and focused so that you can use them to measure the success of your event later on. This list can also guide you as you start the main event planning phases.

2 – Design the Event

The event design phase includes the master plan for your event. You'll start with finding a venue that accommodates the theme of the event, the number of guests, and the purpose of the event. You can work with venue staff throughout the planning process to enhance communication and make sure things run smoothly.
Once you have a location for your event, you can start build a team of people to help you with the remaining design tasks.
Delegating responsibility to different team members allows you to take a management role without becoming too overwhelmed by the details of event planning. Each of your team members will contribute to the master plan.
For example, the person responsible for entertainment will give you a list of performers along with a schedule. The person or group responsible for food and drink will provide a detailed menu along with the associated costs and plan for food service.
Your event design and master plan need to be as detailed as possible to ensure the success of your event.

3 – Brand the Event

A successful event with clear goals and objectives should be easy to brand. You know what the host of the event wants and what guests are expecting. Use your research and your design to brand the event.
But wait! You'll also need to find a way to show how your event is unique and why it's worth attending. You can use promotional materials to bolster the brand and get people talking about your event.

Does your event have a name? Does it have a motto or tagline? These details can make branding your event more successful. Think about a name, tagline, and logo as you form a brand around the event. It should be clear to attendees what they should expect from the event should they choose to attend.

Your branding will help you as you start to publicize the event. You can use an email list, social media posts, or a specific invitation list depending on what the event host has in mind.

4 – Coordination and Day-Of Planning

Your planning is coming together well and you are ready for stage 4 – coordination and day of planning! Coordination refers to finalizing plans with each of your team members and the event staff or volunteers.

Everyone involved with the event should know what is expected of them and how important their role is to event success. You'll need to coordinate the different components of the days event and give the schedule to each team member and your representative at the venue.

The schedule should list each component of the event with a clear start and finish time. You may also include which person or group of people is responsible for each part of the event. You can also include other important information on your day-of schedule such as who to contact if there are technical issues.

This stage is hard work! But it's why event planners are successful – they have impressive attention to detail.

5 – Evaluate the Event

You've made it to the last step of your event planning checklists – the evaluation.

Not all event planners or event planning companies use a formal evaluation. The evaluation stage is useful if you are relatively new to planning or you want to collect positive feedback to build your reputation as a planner.

For conferences and formal work trainings you can send out an online survey or hand out a paper survey to attendees to collect feedback on the event. Include questions about the organization of the event and specific objectives from your list.

But input from attendees is only part of the evaluation. After the event is over you can return to your team's goals and objectives and discuss whether each of those were met. If they were – great! If you think you could have been stronger in a certain area, discuss it. The only way to improve your event planning skills is to be willing to grow and improve.

The 7 Key Event Planning Principles

1. Considering the date
2. Selecting the venue
3. Consulting the budget
4. Defining your objective
5. Deciding how to differentiate yourself
6. Using trusted service providers
7. Having great food

Request for Proposal (RFP) A Request For Proposal (RFP) is a solicitation by an organization to potential suppliers. The buyer is interested in the procurement of services and asks prospective vendors to submit business proposals on a timely basis. The requirements are all the same in order to evaluate responses in a comprehensive and fair manner. Most event organizers send RFPs because they are meeting in a new city and/or do not have an already established track record at a particular venue. They could also just be looking to change due to a flux in meeting requirements. The meeting is significantly larger or smaller, the budget was slashed or the format is being overhauled. Whatever the reason, it is now time to look around. However, be certain you are ready for a change. In other words, it is not ethical to "pit" an established venue you plan to continue using against others.

Typical RFP Structure

1. Introduce your company Start with an overview of your company and what market segment you fall into (corporation, public, charity, association, trade body, etc). You have to appreciate that the person on the other end of your RFP will not have experience of your industry sector so try to summarize exactly what it is you do and who you do business with in layman's terms.

2. Define your event Once you've introduced your company, you will need to carefully define your event's purpose and what you hope to achieve.

What is the aim of the event and what are you hoping to achieve?

Are you looking to host a one off event or are you looking to create a series of regular events?

How often will regular events be held (quarterly, annually, at irregular times)?

If your event is regular will you be looking to host it at different venues or the same one?

Then go onto define your event's profile. Be as clear and as accurate as you can here so the venue has a good idea of what to expect:

Type of event (conference, training, trade show, etc Length of event (an afternoon or a few days?) The number of attendees (try not to underestimate this figure)

Attendee profile (age, gender, nationality, demographic makeup, etc) How your attendees are getting to the venue (driving, flying, public transport, etc)

What will your attendees be doing in their downtime (more relevant to hotels).

3. Set out the dates If possible try to be as flexible as you can on dates, so the venue can review what's available and send you a range of options. These might vary depending on whether they fall in the week or weekend. Mention setup and takedown times as well and try not to underestimate how long this will take. If there is even a small chance you could still be dismantling the day after then make sure you include this.

4. Set out your requirements Make sure to set out your requirements from the outset. These should include: Meeting space required (approximate in square feet/meters) Space required in main event room (approximate in square feet/meters) Number of breakout rooms required Room setup (theatre, round tables and a stage, open floor, booths) The number of exhibitors/vendors you think will be attending and any special requirements Any specific equipment you or exhibitors/vendors will be bringing (large product demos, digital signage) Will you require catering and if so how many meals will you need for how many people? Will you want access to a bar or will you be supplying your own alcohol? Will you need a high quality internet connection? Will you be requiring parking for your attendees? Does the venue offer in-house AV service?

CHAPTER THREE

Event Marketing Advertisements

Event Marketing:

The function of event management that can keep in touch with the event's participants and visitors (consumers), read their needs and motivations, develop products that meet these needs, and build a communication program that expresses the event's purpose and objectives.

In summary, the three features of event marketing are the following:

➢ Intangibility (such as fun, entertainment, and information)

➢ Inseparability (such as the usher's service approach to the customer when the product and provider are inseparable)

➢ Variability (such as different levels of service provided by different ushers or different responses from two or more customers to the same experience

Process of Event Marketing

1. Establish the Features of the Product

Each event offers a range of potential benefits to the event audience. These may include one or more of the following:

➢ a novel experience

➢ Entertainment

➢ a learning experience

➢ an exciting result

➢ an opportunity to meet others

➢ a chance to purchase items

➢ Dining and drinking

➢ an inexpensive way to get out of the house

➢ a chance to see something unique

When marketing an event, therefore, alignment between the product benefits and the needs of the audience is necessary to guide the design of the event and the promotional effort. Pregame and halftime entertainment are good examples of adding value to the main benefit offered by a sporting event product.

2. Identify customers (segmentation)

Customer care is a buzzphrase across all businesses now, particularly service industries like the hospitality trade. It is a major and vital part of event management. Careful consideration needs to be given to all event customers. If they enjoy the event, they will come back themselves and maybe invite their friends to the next part of the program or a future event planned by the same agency.

Market segmentation is the process of analyzing your customers in groups. Some groups may enjoy a particular type of country-and-western music. Others may enjoy line dancing. Yet others might visit just for the excitement and the atmosphere. It is absolutely essential to analyze the different motivations of the event audience and to develop a profile for each of these groups.

3. Plan to Meet Audience Needs

Once you have identified your customer groupings, it is then necessary to ensure that all their needs are met. With the Fan Fair example, there may be a generation of older music enthusiasts who are looking for a certain type of entertainment, as well as a younger group (say aged 10 to 14) who need to be entertained, too, so that they can gain something from the experience.

All audiences need food and facilities, but food and beverage may or may not be a high priority of a particular event audience. For some, the music is the highlight; for others, it is the hype of the event; and for still others, it is the food that is important.

4. Establish the Price and the Ticket Program

The sale and distribution of tickets have been mentioned briefly before now it is necessary to consider that event attendance could be tied to tourist travel to a destination. If this were the case, it would involve negotiations with a tour wholesaler, extending the timeline for planning. Plans would need to be finalized long before the event, with the price determined, brochures printed, and advertising is done (sometimes overseas) well in advance. This package tour might also include airfare and accommodations.

5. Analyze Consumer Decision-Making

The next step is to analyze the customer's decision-making process. Research conducted in this area will produce information that is very useful in guiding promotional efforts.

6. Promote the Event

Having made the decision as to when it is best to promote the event, the next question is how to promote it. Organizers must demonstrate the difference between an event, whether it is a concert, festival, street fair, or charity fun run, from other related leisure options. The consumer needs to know why this event is special.

7. Evaluate Marketing Efforts

The effectiveness of all promotional efforts needs to be carefully monitored. With an annual. The event, for example, customer responses to the various types of promotions will guide promotional efforts in future years. Evaluation needs to be done systematically by asking questions such as "Where did you find out about the event?" or "When did you decide to attend this event?" There are three stages at which research can be conducted: prior to the event, during the event, and after the event. The research can be qualitative, such as focus groups and case studies, or quantitative. In the latter case, the research generates statistics such as customers' expenditures at the event.

Importance of Event Marketing

1. It helps in brand building that is, creating awareness about the launch of new products/brands.
2. To highlight the added features of the product/services.
3. It helps in rejuvenating brands during different stages of the product life cycle.
4. Helping in communicating the repositioning of brands/products.
5. Associating the brand personality of clients with the personality of the target market.
6. Creating and maintaining brand identity.

Out-of-Home Advertising:

Out-of-home media advertising (also OOH advertising or outdoor advertising) or out-of-home media (also OOH media or outdoor media) is advertising that reaches consumers while they are outside their homes.

Out-of-home media advertising is focused on marketing to consumers when they are "on the go" in public places, in transit, waiting (such as in a medical office), and/or in specific commercial locations (such as in a retail venue). OOH advertising formats fall into six main categories:

- Billboard Advertising
- Point of Sale displays
- Street furniture (Bus shelters, Kiosks, Telephone booths, etc)
- Transit advertising and wraps (taxis, buses, subways, trains, etc)
- Mobile billboards

Types of Billboards

1. Classic or Bulletin Billboards- Classic billboards have been used for the purpose of advertising for a long period of time. These billboards are usually large in size and are most popularly known as bulletin boards. They are used on highways as well as streets where a significant number of people can see them. This includes both pedestrians as well as people in their vehicles. The size of these billboards has increased with time due to the increase in the speed of motorized vehicles. As a result, people in moving vehicles can easily read through the advertised message without slowing down their vehicles. Classic billboards can be found in different sizes such as 14′ high x 48′ wide, 10.5′ high x 36′ wide, etc.

2. Vinyl Billboards- Vinyl billboards are bright in color and are usually spray painted with UV-resistant paint. It has a life of three to five years and the material used is known as polyvinyl chloride. They are digitally painted banners made with the help of large inkjet printers. Vinyl banners are most commonly used as company logos or for special events.

3. Painted Billboards - These billboards are very rare these days as they have been replaced by graphically printed billboards. Painted billboards are basically done by manually painting the advertised message and images on the billboards.

4. Mobile Billboards- Mobile billboards are used where the target audience is present at a large event. The billboard is placed on top of a moving vehicle so, it can be seen wherever the vehicle moves. Mobile billboards are beneficial if you want to move your billboards from one place to another, unlike other static billboards.

5. Three-dimensional- Billboards These are the latest type of billboards that catch the eye of onlookers and are very artistic. They are designed in such a way that the image pops out and the emphasis on the product is more. For example, if you are advertising a new dish, you can make the dish pop out using this billboard so that there is more emphasis on the product

rather than the rest of the billboard.

6. Scented Billboards - These billboards are extremely rare and are used to pass the scent of the product. For example, if you are advertising your new restaurant dish, then you can use a scented billboard so that passersby can get the smell and be persuaded to enter your restaurant.

7. Digital Billboards- Digital billboards are used generally at central business points to ensure they are seen by a maximum number of people. As a result, it provides maximum brand exposure. These billboards can also be seen displaying stock market prices or displaying the temperature in some places. They are expensive but are also very effective at catching the attention of people and thus, promoting your business.

CHAPTER FOUR

BASIC EVENT ACCOUNTING IN EVENT MANAGEMENT

Definition

An event budget is an estimation of the costs an event will incur based on plans made as well as research. Whether you are planning a small event or a large sophisticated one, your corporate event cannot exceed your budget.

How to Create an Event Planning Budget

The best event planning occurs when organizers utilize the wide array of tools available to them. A few important steps are necessary after including aspects of the event in the event plan template. Create the best event plan by choosing an event template that helps you achieve the following:

- Prepare for Adjustments

A budget template is very much like writing a book. The process may require major adjustments, resulting in several drafts. The best templates enable organizers to make these adjustments as often as is necessary whether before, during, after, or in between events.

- Improve Budget over Time

Researching expenditures, for instance regarding a choice of venue, may take time. Your template should include features that ensure flexibility. This will event planners improve the budget as time goes by or as they access details that they may not have known at the beginning of the budget planning process. Using an event ROI tool is helpful to get a comprehensive view of the value of your event—this will come in handy when you are quantifying your event and figuring out future budgets.

- Always Include a Contingency Plan

The inclusion of a contingency plan helps a corporate event planner prepare for the things that may go wrong. It's basically a written commitment to planning for the unexpected. For instance, what will you do if your outdoor event is suddenly threatened by an unexpected thunderstorm?

Aspects of the event budget

Event planning can be a challenging affair, especially when it comes to the budget. There's simply so much to consider and prepare. That's why every corporate event planner needs a planning budget. This will help you prepare for every aspect of the event and ensure you save instead of overspending. By using an event budget template, you'll be able to plan in detail and prepare for the unexpected. Make the best choices as you prepare for your event by using a budget plan template that includes the following:

- Travel & Accommodation

Will your corporation need to provide accommodation for anyone who will attend the event? If so, how much will this cost? Though this can be an overlooked aspect of your budget, depending on the size and grandeur of the event, be sure to place this estimation at the forefront of your budget to avoid underestimating the finances you'll need to make your event a success.

- Food

How much will food cost? This will depend on the number of people you expect to attend as well as how extensive the menu will be. Estimate costs according to the scale and type of event you are organizing.

- Staff Compensation

To avoid financial difficulties that may arise due to a poorly budgeted event, also include staff compensation in your event plan template. Event directors or managers will need to determine how many staff members will be required to organize and help facilitate a successful event. Determine how much time will be spent and the appropriate compensation required.

- Facility Expenses

Facility expenses include money spent on acquiring the venue. Make a budget based on what you think would be a likely cost. Also consider hidden costs that may arise such as costs associated with security, lighting, or heating.

- Logistics

Do you need special contracts, permits, or insurance in hosting your event? Each of these considerations falls under logistics, an important aspect of any budget. Your ability to estimate how much this will cost will depend mainly on the venue of your corporate event.

- Marketing & PR

Marketing is an important aspect of any event. It can account for a significant percentage of your corporate event budget as well especially when organizers expect to gain profits through event entrance fees or other charges. Consider the tools you intend to use to market your event and make your choices based on which are most aligned with your budget.

Fixed and Variable Costs

It's also crucial to differentiate between fixed and variable expenses or costs. Fixed costs are costs that do not change based on the number of attendees. These costs are calculated as a total amount. Variable costs are costs that change based on the number of attendees. These costs are calculated on a per-person basis.

Event Budget Expenses

Let's go over the basic categories of expenses that apply to nearly every event. Consider these carefully as you prepare your budget.

1. The Venue

The venue is usually the largest expense in any event budget. Most event planners choose their venue before they make other purchases or commit to other vendors.

Since the venue is the most impactful component of your event, its cost will likely determine what you can spend on everything else.

Additionally, your venue will also have the most impact on your budget. For instance, if the venue provides food, you can eliminate that line from your budget. But if the venue doesn't provide wait staff, you may need to hire your own. So once you choose a venue, you'll inevitably have to revisit your budget to make changes.

Selecting a venue is a big process, so take it seriously. Make sure you understand its real costs. Many venues have a schedule of additional fees on top of the advertised price. For instance, they might charge a clean up fee or a security fee.

It's also important to understand exactly what you get for your money. Many venues have a menu of additional services, like valet attendants, Wi-

Fi, or specialized equipment. Don't assume anything comes with the base price. Make sure your contract details everything.

2. Speakers or Entertainment

Depending on your needs, entertainment could be a big or small expense. If all you need is a DJ for the day, you won't invest much. But if you need a high-profile keynote speaker or popular music act, you may end up spending as much on entertainment as you spent on the venue.

Like your venue, this is a component that reaches beyond today's event. Your attendees will talk about the entertainment. Great entertainment won't just drive signups for today's event. Word will spread and create buzz for your next event too. So don't be afraid to spend on quality.

3. Staffing

Your venue may include your general staffing needs, but you may need some specialized people to handle complex tasks like registration, organization, and managing speakers and/or entertainment. Expect to compensate good help for their labor, travel expenses, accommodations, and meals.

4. Signage and Branding

Creating a powerful event experience means bringing your brand to life. To do that, you'll need to include branded elements throughout your venue.

This is one of the places of your budget where it's easy to overspend, so it's important to have a clear vision in mind before you start buying visual elements. You wouldn't, for instance, want to spend a load of cash on a waterfall feature and then run out of money to label the bathrooms.

HubSpot's INBOUND event takes branding to the next level with giant 3-D signs and high-quality displays scattered throughout the entire venue. They use artwork to inform and amaze their guests.

5. Technology Expenses

Most modern events use technology in some way to enhance the experience (especially video). You may need microphones and PA systems, televisions or projectors, digital signage, or a custom event app to create a truly engaging experience for your attendees.

Start by making a list of the different types of technology you'll need for your event. For instance, if you plan to have a single speaker at any given time, you'll need at least one computer and screen for their display equipment.

Next, make some calls to get an idea of how much that equipment would cost for rental and setup. Depending on your needs, you may want to hire a contractor to manage the pieces.

6. Promotional Expenses

Planning the event includes marketing it. You'll need to decide how much you're willing to spend to attract people to register and attend your event. How you attract attendees will depend on your event and audience. If you're planning a company picnic, marketing might be as simple as sending a few emails to the company email list, announcing it over the PA system, or asking managers to hand out flyers to their teams. In these cases, your expenses would be pretty low.

If you're throwing an industry conference, however, you may invest more in marketing. You might choose to use email marketing, blogging, paid ads, press releases, and affiliates to get the word out. In these cases, your promotional expenses would add up quickly.

7. Emergency Fund

No matter how carefully you budget every detail of your event, it's critical to set aside some cash as an emergency fund. Undoubtedly, you'll have a few last-minute expenses you can't avoid.

Here are some examples of instances where you might need an emergency fund:

- A speaker cancels, so you have to find someone at the last minute (expensive).
- After setting up, you realize you don't have enough signage to help your guests get around.
- A vendor fails to deliver a food ingredient, so you have to order something else.

If any of those instances occurred during your event, a stash of cash would literally save your event. Set 10% to 20% of your total budget aside for emergencies.

8. Food Expenses

If the venue you choose won't cater your event, you'll need a separate line item for food.

Fortunately, food is a special category because you have a lot of control over what you serve. There are always ways to raise or lower the cost of this expense. If another budget item goes over, you'll most likely be able to make adjustments to your food budget to compensate.

Most caterers will give you a price per guest to help you plan meals. Total your guests, speakers, volunteers, staff, and anyone else who's a part of your event, then add 10% for incidentals.

9. Gifts

It's smart to send every attendee home with something in their hand. Some events give their guests small tokens like pens, keychains, or stickers. Other events give their attendees gift bags worth hundreds of dollars.

You may want to give different gifts to different people depending on their roles. For instance, a keynote speaker would receive a nicer gift than a volunteer or someone who purchased your cheapest admission ticket.

10. Other Expenses

Every event is different, so we can't predict exactly what your event needs. The previous categories apply to every event, but here are a few less common expenses you might incur:

? Equipment rentals (tables, chairs, bars, tents, attractions, stages, lighting, audio/visual, etc.)

? Printing (invitations, schedules, programs, badges, etc.)

? Costumes, uniforms, or specialized clothing

? Security

? On-site medical services

? Cosmetic services (hair, makeup, manicures, pedicures, etc.)

? Activities (golf, spa, demonstrations, games, etc.)

? Software and apps

? Permits and licenses

? Gratuities

? Transportation (moving equipment or people around)

? Insurance

? Legal Fees

Expenses for Virtual Events

For a fully customized and branded virtual event, there are three common expenses that planners should consider budgeting for:

1. The virtual event platform you'll host your event in
2. Design of your virtual event space
3. Your streaming service

Funding For an Event

1. Crowdfunding

The advent of crowdfunding platforms like Kick starter has made testing the appetite for new events so much easier, allowing organizers to try out ideas before risking cash. You simply provide details about your great, new event, set a fundraising target, and ask wannabe attendees to pledge to buy a ticket if the event takes place. If there is not sufficient interest and you don't meet your target then the pledged money is released.

Therefore, it is a risk-free 'investment' for the attendees and also for the organizer, who does not need to stake their own funds. However, although the process is simple, attracting ticket purchasers is not necessarily as easy. You will need to hit up everyone you know to spread the word about your campaign, launch an assault on social media and dedicate much time and resources to marketing.

2. Angel Investor

Angel investors are wealthy individuals or groups of people looking for investment opportunities.

Other routes to finding an investor would be approaching existing contacts who know and trust you or highly targeted individual investors or specialist investment groups. For example, if you want to launch a conference about innovations in cleantech, approach an investor with a track record in energy, not someone who usually places their money in real estate, for example.

3. Savings/ internal marketing budget

Also known as the 'put your money where your mouth is' option! Look at your own resources to see how much cash you personally or your company can put into the budget. Exposing yourself to some level of risk can demonstrate your commitment and help encourage other investors, sponsors and partners to get on board.

4. Bank loan

Banks don't hand out loans as easily as they once did, and they are unlikely to lend against an event itself, but if you have a company with a proven track record, a business loan may be an option. Alternatively, you can borrow against an existing asset, such as your house, but unless you are 100% certain your event will be a success you will have to give this one a lot of thought before committing.

5. Advance ticket sales

Using an event-ticketing platform like Eventbrite you can start selling tickets long in advance of your planned event date. Not only does this enable you to test the water as to the desirability of your event idea, it also gives you access to some working capital. If you're organizing an event that's using Eventbrite Payment Processing, you're qualified to apply for Advance Payment to receive payment before your event takes place.

Twice a month, you can receive a proportion of your advance ticket sales, supplying you with vital cash flow to get your project off the ground.

6. Sponsorship

Corporate sponsorship is a very effective way to fund key elements of your event and is utilized by the vast majority of events. However, sponsors usually come on board after your event has gotten off the drawing board. Sponsors will want to know how many people are coming to your event, when and where it's taking place, what's on the agenda and see your marketing plan.

It will probably be necessary to get some core funding in place – or have people already signed up for your event – before approaching sponsors. When you do, make sure you have also finalized your sponsorship packages and are clear on exactly what benefits you can offer to sponsors.

7. Sale of exhibition space

In the same way, you can sell tickets in advance of your event, you can also pre-sell exhibition stands and take deposits from exhibitors. You can sell space for hundreds of pounds per square meter so you can raise a significant chunk of capital by getting exhibitors on board early. However, being a new show with no track record will make securing exhibitors a challenge.

Work your existing contacts to gain your first few exhibitors, offering them tempting early bird discounts. You can then use their commitment to helping convince others of the credibility of your event.

8. Barter

Finally, don't discount the value of in-kind funding. What can you or your company offer to companies in return for the goods and services you need? For example, a magazine that is organising a reader event could offer a catering company free print advertising in exchange for providing f&b.

Alternatively, you can offer partners the opportunity to play a role at the event itself – e.g. negotiate with the venue to give you a discount if you allow them to make a presentation.

Steps to balance event budget

1. Focus on your event strategy and goals

Before diving into the event budget, it's important to lock down a strong event strategy. Without one, it can be difficult to make key choices to shape your budget. An event strategy will encompass your overall vision for the event, along with goals and objectives on how to get there.

2. Document your core event costs

Some of your costs will be determined by the format of your event. For instance, a virtual event won't necessarily require on-site health and safety

measures, but an in-person one might Other in-person and hybrid event cost categories can include:
? Food and beverage
? Venue and rentals
? Signage and decor
? Travel and lodging
? On-site check-in and badges
? A/V and live streaming services
* Include a contingency budget
When setting your ballpark budget, add some extra cushion — around 10-20% — to serve as your emergency fund. This way, if an unexpected cost comes up, you'll already be covered.
3. Make room for event marketing
It's difficult to host a successful event without buzz. The revenue generated from ticket sales is often the main driver of income, so budgeting to get the word out will be an important step. Whether that's through social media, design, or traditional advertising, your budget must include a space for promotion and marketing.
4. Add in experiential extras
If you seek to create surprise-and-delight moments and deeper emotional connections with your attendees, you'll need your budget planning to include experiential marketing.
Experiential events can be small and intimate or large and loud, but it's the thought and detail behind the investment that makes the difference. Contests and giveaways, Celebrity appearances, Materials for workshops, Yoga, meditation, or mixology classes, and VIP accommodations are the examples. 5. Factor in your technology
Whether your event is onsite, virtual, or hybrid, you'll need event technology to support it. Look for an event platform that eliminates additional expenses to drive efficiencies. Ideally, you will want to find a virtual or hybrid platform with the following features and integrations:
- Integrated event websites: You definitely need a landing page for your event. Seek out platforms that automatically integrate with event registration and tracking rather than paying a web developer to design something for you.
- Registration tools: A common need is custom registration flows and forms, ideally self-coded.
- Email communications: Email marketing can drive $36 of revenue for

every $1 invested. Whether you use email to publicize your event or just to communicate with attendees, you'll need software to help you write, design, send, and track emails.

- Virtual sponsor booths: Your sponsors signed up for your event for a reason, whether that was to collect leads or improve brand recognition. It is thus important to make sure they have a platform that's engaging and customizable.
- Online venue for attendees: A well-designed virtual venue can be just as engaging as a physical one, and can level the playing field for virtual attendees at hybrid events by giving them a space that facilitates exploration, networking, and engagement.

6. Capitalize on revenue opportunities

With the budget starting to turn into a fair estimation of actual costs, it's time to look at the potential revenue sources to balance it out.

First, consider paid tickets.

- Ticket sales can be boosted by offering different ticket types:
- Early bird discounts: Play into the sense of urgency by offering a better deal if attendees buy before anyone else. It's worth offering a steep discount to have a locked-in, engaged audience.
- VIP or premium add-ons: Creating extra value lets you charge extra for tickets. This can be in the form of one-on-one sessions with your expert speakers, a special cocktail hour for VIPs only, or luxe accommodations.
- Referral programs: With the help of referral software, you can turn your attendees into brand ambassadors, offering them a discount on their own ticket for referring friends.

Second, you can look for sponsors to offset costs or become profitable.

7. Become an event ROI rock star

By now, you should feel confident about this process. You're long past base camp — you're close to the top of your event-budgeting mountain.

All you need to reach the summit is to calculate the ROI of your event.

To calculate ROI, follow this simple formula:

[(Total Revenue) ÷ Total Cost of the Event] = ROI

Run the numbers. If you come up with a 1, you've broken even on your event. Seeing a 2 or 3 means you've generated a profit that's two-to-three times your costs.

For example, your ROI from a tech conference with paid tickets and sales might look like:

[($10,000 in ticket sales + $100,000 in sponsorships + $2,500 in merch sales) ÷ ($80,000 total expenditure on event)] = 1.4

An ROI of 1.4 means that for every $1 invested in your event, you got $1.40 back

CHAPTER FIVE

EVENT SAFETY AND SECURITY

Risk

Risk is a combination of harm and the likelihood that it will occur.

The main harms that event owners face is:

1 Injuries to persons

2 Damage to property

3 Adverse business impact such as a loss of revenue or increased operating costs

4 Higher insurance premiums due to claims and lawsuits

5 Event disruptions such as late or cancelled showings stemming from security threats

6 Inadequate venue capacity and services such as food, parking, and toilet facility's & traffic control leading to patron dissatisfaction and the potential for escalation

7 Loss of reputation as sponsors, vendors, patrons & fans may not attend future events.

Pre-event planning should begin well before the date of the event to allow sufficient time to address all threat potentials and develop effective plans to prevent them. Often months are required for proper planning. Planning should include key partners such as private security firms, law enforcement agencies, fire departments, emergency medical services (EMS), transportation departments, public works, health and public agencies, vendors and businesses participating in the event. Clear leadership, designated responsibilities and communication need to be established between all partners as well as their role in the event of an emergency. Assistance from multiple agencies may be needed even when one law enforcement agency clearly has the lead and provides most of the resources. An example would be the fire department at a festival in a city park.

Recent criminal attacks have shown the importance of proper event safety and security planning, and the value of effective emergency response. Sporting events, fairs, festivals, concerts, conferences, fund raisers, political campaigns, and exhibitions, by their very nature attract crowds and may also become targets for crimes such as theft, robbery, assault and terrorism. These events become bigger targets as crowds assemble and grow. They may also become opportunities for special interest groups to publicly demonstrate. Poor event planning, management, crowd control, security, and ineffective emergency response, increase the likelihood of injuries, property damage and even catastrophic attacks. Proper event safety and security must be tailored to each specific event and potential exposure. This Loss Control Alert provides a framework to support safety and security planning by offering a series of topic-specific questions. Answers to these questions will assist in crafting an effective safety and security plan.

Essentials of event security

- Invest is complete venue security
- Educate your teamKnow the people who work for you
- Don't forget cyber security
- Have crowd management measures in place
- Keep medical staff on hand
- Draft an emergency preparedness plan
- attendees can be threats too

Risk management is an important topic in event planning because failing to recognize potential problems can have a huge impact on many areas of your business, including your reputation and financial stability

Reasons of risk

- Equipment or power failure
- Medical emergencies
- Sponsor withdrawal
- Fires and floods
- Last-minute cancellations
- Food safety concerns
- Severe weather or natural disasters, and finally
- Financial troubles

Risk Management Process

The risk management process is a framework for the actions that need to be taken. There are five basic steps that are taken to manage risk; these steps are referred to as the risk management process. It begins with identifying risks, goes on to analyze risks, then the risk is prioritized, a solution is implemented, and finally, the risk is monitored. In manual systems, each step involves a lot of documentation and administration.

Here Are the Five Essential Steps of a Risk Management Process

1. Identify the Risk
2. Analyze the Risk
3. Evaluate or Rank the Risk
4. Treat the Risk
5. Monitor and Review the Risk

Step 1: Identify the Risk

The initial step in the risk management process is to identify the risks that the business is exposed to in its operating environment.

There are many different types of risks:

- Legal risks
- Environmental risks
- Market risks
- Regulatory risks etc.

It is important to identify as many of these risk factors as possible. In a manual environment, these risks are noted down manually. If the organization has a risk management solution employed all this information is inserted directly into the system.

The advantage of this approach is that these risks are now visible to every stakeholder in the organization with access to the system. Instead of this vital information being locked away in a report which has to be requested via email, anyone who wants to see which risks have been identified can access the information in the risk management system.

Step 2: Analyze the Risk

Once a risk has been identified it needs to be analyzed. The scope of the risk must be determined. It is also important to understand the link between the risk and different factors within the organization. To determine the severity and seriousness of the risk it is necessary to see how many business functions the risk affects. There are risks that can bring the whole business to a standstill if actualized, while there are risks that will only be minor inconveniences in the analysis.

Step 3: Evaluate the Risk or Risk Assessment

Risks need to be ranked and prioritized. Most risk management solutions have different categories of risks, depending on the severity of the risk. A risk that may cause some inconvenience is rated lowly, risks that can result in catastrophic loss are rated the highest. It is important to rank risks because it allows the organization to gain a holistic view of the risk exposure of the whole organization. The business may be vulnerable to several low-level risks, but it may not require upper management intervention. On the other hand, just one of the highest-rated risks is enough to require immediate intervention.

Step 4: Treat the Risk

Every risk needs to be eliminated or contained as much as possible. This is done by connecting with the experts of the field to which the risk belongs. In a manual environment, this entails contacting each and every stakeholder and then setting up meetings so everyone can talk and discuss the issues. The problem is that the discussion is broken into many different email threads, across different documents and spreadsheets, and many different phone calls. In a risk management solution, all the relevant stakeholders can be sent notifications from within the system. The discussion regarding the risk and its possible solution can take place from within the system. Upper management can also keep a close eye on the solutions being suggested and the progress being made within the system. Instead of everyone contacting each other to get updates, everyone can get updates directly from within the risk management solution.

Step 5: Monitor and Review the Risk

Not all risks can be eliminated – some risks are always present. Market risks and environmental risks are just two examples of risks that always need to be monitored. Under manual systems monitoring happens through diligent employees. These professionals must make sure that they keep a close watch on all risk factors. Under a digital environment, the risk management system monitors the entire risk framework of the organization. If any factor or risk changes, it is immediately visible to everyone. Computers are also much better at continuously monitoring risks than people. Monitoring risks also allows your business to ensure continuity

NDMA Guidelines for Crowd Management NDMA Guidelines: NDMA had released an elaborate document for integrated crowd management. As per this document, the integrated crowd management is based on several pillars such as capacity planning, risk assessment, improved preparedness planning, incidence response, capacity building etc. The planning and management is subjective based on several parameters such as –

? Type of event (such as religious, schools/ university, sports event, music event, political event, product promotion etc.)

? Expected Crowd (age, gender, economic strata etc. such as farmers, shopkeepers)

? Crowd Motives (such as social, academic, religious, entertainment, economic etc.)

? Venue (location, topography of area, temporal or permanent, open or closed, public or private)

? Role of other stake holders (such as NGOs, neighbours of event venue, local administrators etc)

Some salient points from the NDMA guidelines are as follows:

? Crowd Queues : Initial focus should be on traffic regulations around the mass gathering venues. There should be a route map for venues along with emergency exits route maps. Also, there should be Barricade facility to control the movement of crowd queues. In case of large crowd gathering, there should be snake line approach, along with constant monitoring of crowds for developing hazard points.

? VIPs: There should be specific plans to handle VIPs and if VIPs add the security concerns then authorities should refuse entry to VIPs.

? Communications: There should be CCTV surveillance, along with another public address system, such as loudspeakers should be installed at all crowded points, in order to communicate with the crowds.

? Medical facilities: Ambulance and health care professionals should be available on venues. NDMA has recommended the medical first-aid rooms and emergency operations in order to handle post-disaster emergencies.

? Basic facilities: The venue organisers should ensure authorised use of electricity, fire safety extinguishers and other arrangements as per the safety guidelines.

Event organizers: Event organizers and venue managers should prepare and review the disaster management plan by coordinating with local administration and police. This will ensure that all the necessary facilities such as transport, medical and emergency facilities are as per safety standards.

? Civil society : Police authorities should access the preparedness. Also, Event/venue managers should involve NGOs and civil society in traffic control, medical assistance and mobilization of local resources in case of disaster.

? Capacity building : In order to be proactive, there is need to focus on the capacity building. Also, the training manual should be periodically in order to usher in new crowd management technique. Apart from that if there is issue of insufficient Security personnel, students, NGOs and civil society should be roped in. Also, the media should be trained to manage communications during crowd disasters.

Crowd Manager

A Crowd Manager is an individual that has been trained and certified by the Fire Prevention Office in safety practices and crowd management techniques.

Functions of security

- Check security passes for individuals entering property
- Ensure and deliver receipts and other valuable items
- Investigate and report evidence to clients for court case preparations
- Maintain the order on properties or in large groups
- Monitor security systems and be ready to alert authorities
- Offer advice on better security services for clients
- Offer directions to authorized guests
- Patrol properties and ensure that all points of entry are secure
- Watch for safety hazards

Safety Plan

Event safety, in a traditional sense, meant safe rigging and production practices, but today, it also includes public health concerns, data privacy, and using event technology to mitigate any event risks.

Need of safety plan.

1. Health and Safety Risk Assessment

The complexity of the event will determine the length and thoroughness of your health and safety risk assessment. For a simple soiree, a standard risk assessment is sufficient, addressing specific issues that may arise at the event - that would endanger any staff, any people attending the event, and any members of the public/anyone who could be impacted.

2. Measures to Alleviate the Risks

Alleviating and managing risk at your event involves identifying what could go wrong - within reason - and putting measures in place to make sure those risks are lessened or eliminated, if possible. When your chefs are working in a new kitchen, the head chef and a qualified risk manager must examine the new workspace to make sure that all of the equipment is up to the appropriate safety standards. On the other hand, if food is being brought from an offsite location, the risks associated with moving food have to be considered instead. Also events may now require staff to wear a facemask and gloves while working in their specific environment. If this is the case, make sure you and your staff always follow the business guidelines around when to wear them and replace them.

3. Develop an Emergency Plan

Every event safety plan needs an emergency plan in case there's need to evacuate, in case of a fire, or any other circumstances. You want to train staff on what to do in case of emergency, decide who will take action, how you will let people know about the emergency (i.e. radio, mobile phones, coded messages), who will make statements about the incident to the authorities and emergency services. You'll also need a contingency plan as part of your safety manual. The contingency plan should be discussed with the emergency services, they should have a copy, and everything should be well-documented. They will need to know, for example, the number of guests and staff and their names, if possible, as well as contact details for each. For lesser emergencies, there needs to be a first aid kit (or several) on site too.

4. Food Safety Considerations

Whether your chefs and caterers are cooking in a new kitchen or bringing food on site, the event safety plan should include detail on how you'll ensure that food does not fall into the temperature danger-zone (4-60°C) which could compromise the safety of guests. You'll also want to know that food will be prepared safely in a hygienic environment, but also in an environment that is safe for the staff. For example, are there slip-resistant mats in place to prevent slips in the kitchens and hallways, or do those need to be brought in externally? Everything to do with bringing the food to the guests' plates should be considered - how it will get there, who will carry it, what dangers does every step present, and so forth? Along with creating a safe work environment, it's important to maintain extremely high hygiene standards. When you're working with food, work surfaces and all kitchen utensils need to be clean and steps must be put in place to avoid cross contamination. Also as you're dealing with food and utensils and potentially customers, it's really important that all staff keep washing and sterilising their hands regularly to avoid possible cross contamination.

5. Crowd Management

When there are large crowds of people, safety can be compromised, so your event safety plan needs to include a way to control crowds. For example, if there are tickets sold at the door, how will you move people through the gates quickly enough not to cause a bottleneck? How will you manage large influxes of people in certain areas? Will areas be spaced out so that there are stations to make sure that people do not all gather in the same areas? Make sure you have a plan for making sure that guests go where they should and that there are no back doors or gates that allow people to go outside the event area where they could potentially be injured.

6. A Parking Plan

Even the best events can be ruined by insufficient or badly managed parking. For any large event (or even small ones), there needs to be a reliable parking plan. You'll need to know approximately how many cars will need to be parked and how you will manage traffic throughout the day(s). Poorly-managed parking has the potential to frustrate and even injure guests and staff if any accidents occur.

If you are charging for parking spaces, you'll have an exact number of spaces reserved before the event, but if you aren't planning on charging for spaces - patrons should still be asked to reserve a free parking spot. This way both you and your attendees know if they can / cannot drive to the event.

7. Appropriate Training for All Staff

Once your event safety plan is in place, you should train staff on both safety procedures and their specific roles at the event ahead of time. Everyone should know what they are doing when and which risks they'll be exposed to at every step of the way. Make sure that staff are well-trained in the event of an emergency and that they know how to follow a clear safety procedure if required. Event management policies

An event management policy is one of several generic rule types that perform actions against events that meet selection criteria specified in an associated event selector. An event management policy selects the events that you want to process, defines the processes needed to manage those events, and schedules when the events are processed.

Event management policies can be defined interactively by using predefined, out-of-the-box policy types accessed through the console. You can also create new user-defined policy types to add new event processing actions.

Whether predefined or user-defined, all event management policies consist of the following attributes:

? Event selector

? Process(es)
? Timeframe(s)
? Evaluation order

Event Management Process/procedure 1. Set ROI-Driven Event Goals and Objectives

ROI-driven events start with setting the right goals and objectives. Goals form the foundation of your event strategy and guide your planning. Goals and objectives also help you define your key metrics and benchmarks to measure performance. Your goals should also be specific and measurable. Setting an event goal of generating leads is too vague. Quantify your goal and add a time limit. Your goals should also be specific and measurable. Setting an event goal of generating leads is too vague. Quantify your goal and add a time limit. 2. Create a Solid Event Budget

Creating an event budget is critical. Not only will it help you avoid overspending, but it will give you a clearer picture of what you need to prove ROI. While the budget stage does not require deep planning, you'll need to map out an initial plan or checklist that lists all of your event components. It's also one of the first tasks of the event management process because it's how you allocate the necessary resources for your event components. 3. Design and Plan a Memorable Event

4. Coordinate the Day of the Event

To ensure event-day success, create a minute-by-minute event walkthrough for your internal teams that specifies each activity and team responsibility. The walkthrough is a final checklist that covers logistical details, roles, assignments, and event scheduling. 5. Evaluate Your Event's Performance and Power Future Events

Below are some factors you might want to dig into:

? Your event goals
? Forecasting goals
? Other KPIs / metrics
? Sponsor impressions
? Attendee impressions
? Event committee performance

Some of these will require you to export data from your event management platform or event software. You can also evaluate more qualitative data like attendee and sponsor feedback, and responses to post-event surveys.

CHAPTER SIX

Leadership & Team Management

Crisis:
A crisis can occur as a result of an unpredictable event or an unforeseeable consequence of some event that had been considered a potential risk.

Crisis Management
Crisis management is the application of strategies designed to help an organization deal with a sudden and significant negative event.

Stages of a crisis
1. Warning and risk assessment.
As important as it may be to identify risks and plan for ways to minimize those risks and their effects, it is equally important to establish monitoring systems that can provide early warning signals of any foreseeable crisis. These early warning systems can take a variety of forms and differ widely based on the identified risks.
Some early warning systems might be mechanical or electronic. For instance, thermography is sometimes used to detect a build-up of heat before a fire starts. Other early warning systems may consist of financial metrics. For example, an organization might be able to anticipate a substantial drop in revenue by monitoring its customers' stock prices.
2. Crisis response and management.
When a crisis occurs, the crisis manager is responsible for directing the organization's response in accordance with its established crisis management plan. The crisis manager is usually also the person who is tasked with communicating with the public.

If a crisis affects public health or safety, then the crisis manager should make a public statement as quickly as possible. In a public crisis, the media will inevitably seek out employees for comment. It is important for the organization's employees to know ahead of time who is and is not authorized to speak to the media. Employees who are allowed to speak to the media must do so in a manner consistent with what the crisis manager is saying.

3. Post-crisis and resolution.

After a crisis subsides and business begins to return to normal, the crisis manager should continue to meet with members of the crisis management team, especially those from the legal and finance departments, to evaluate the progression of the recovery efforts. At the same time, the crisis manager will need to provide the latest information to key stakeholders to keep them aware of the current situation.

Following a crisis, it is also important for the crisis management team to revisit the organization's crisis management plan with the goal of evaluating how well the plan worked and what aspects of the plan need to be revised based on what was learned during the crisis.

Characteristics of Crisis

? A crisis is a sequence of sudden disturbing events harming the organization.

? The crisis generally arises on short notice.

? A crisis triggers a feeling of fear and threat among the individuals, Crisis can arise in an organization due to any of the following reasons:

? Technological failure and Breakdown of machines lead to crisis. Problems in the internet, corruption in the software, and errors in passwords all result in crises.

? A crisis arises when employees do not agree with each other and fight amongst themselves. A crisis arises as a result of boycotts, strikes for indefinite periods, disputes, and so on.

? Violence, thefts, and terrorism at the workplace result in organizational crises.

? Neglecting minor issues, in the beginning, can lead to a major crisis and a situation of uncertainty at the workplace. The management must have complete control over its employees and should not adopt a casual attitude at work.

? Illegal behaviors such as accepting bribes, fraud, data, or information tampering all lead to organizational crises.

? A crisis arises when an organization fails to pay its creditors and declares itself a bankrupt organization

Need for Crisis Management

? Crisis Management prepares individuals to face unexpected developments and adverse conditions in the organization with courage and determination.

? Employees adjust well to sudden changes in the organization.

? Employees can understand and analyze the causes of the crisis and cope with it in the best possible way.

? Crisis Management helps managers to devise strategies to come out of uncertain conditions and also decide on the future course of action.

? Crisis Management helps managers to feel the early signs of crisis, warn the employees against the aftermath and take necessary precautions for the same.

Essential Features of Crisis Management

? Crisis Management includes activities and processes which help the managers as well as employees to analyze and understand events that might lead to crisis and uncertainty in the organization.

? Crisis Management enables managers and employees to respond effectively to changes in the organization's culture.

? It consists of effective coordination amongst the departments to overcome emergency situations.

? Employees in times of crisis must communicate effectively with each other and try their level best to overcome tough times.

Types of Crisis Following are the types of crises:

1. Natural Crisis Disturbances in the environment and nature lead to natural crises. Such events are generally beyond the control of human beings. Tornadoes, Earthquakes, Hurricanes, Landslides, Tsunamis, floods, and Drought all result in a natural disaster.

2. Technological Crisis - Technological crisis arises as a result of failure in technology. Problems in the overall systems lead to technological crises. The breakdown of machines, corrupted software, and so on give rise to the technological crisis.

3. Confrontation Crisis - Confrontation crises arise when employees fight amongst themselves. Individuals do not agree with each other and eventually depend on non-productive acts like boycotts, strikes for indefinite periods, and so on. In such a type of crisis, employees disobey

superiors; give them ultimatums and force them to accept their demands. Internal disputes, ineffective communication, and lack of coordination give rise to confrontation crises.

4. Crisis of Malevolence - Organizations face a crisis of malevolence when some notorious employees take the help of criminal activities and extreme steps to fulfill their demands. Acts like kidnapping company officials and false rumors all lead to a crisis of malevolence.

5. Crisis of Organizational Misdeeds- Crises of organizational misdeeds arise when management takes certain decisions knowing the harmful consequences of the same towards the stakeholders and external parties. In such cases, superiors ignore the after-effects of strategies and implement the same for quick results.

6. Crisis due to Workplace Violence - Such a type of crisis arises when employees are indulged in violent acts such as beating employees, and superiors on the office premises itself.

7. Crisis Due to Rumors - Spreading false rumors about the organization and brand leads to crisis. Employees must not spread anything which would tarnish the image of their organization.

8. Bankruptcy - A crisis also arises when organizations fail to pay their creditors and other parties. Lack of funds leads to crisis.

9. Crisis Due to Natural Factors - Disturbances in the environment and nature such as hurricanes, volcanoes, storms, floods; droughts, earthquakes, etc result in crisis.

10. Sudden Crisis - As the name suggests, such situations arise all of a sudden and on extremely short notice. Managers do not get warning signals and such a situation is in most cases beyond anyone's control.

11. Smoldering Crisis Neglecting minor issues, in the beginning, lead to a smoldering crisis later. Managers often can foresee crises but they should not ignore the same and wait for someone else to take action. Warn the employees immediately to avoid such a situation.

What is a Crisis Management Plan?

Individuals need to adopt a step-by-step approach during critical situations. Planning is essential. Getting hyper does not solve any problem, instead makes the situation worse. It is a crime to take impulsive and hasty decisions during a crisis. It is essential to think rationally and devise strategies that would work best during emergency situations. Complaining and cribbing lead you nowhere. A crisis Management Plan refers to a detailed plan which describes the various actions which need to be taken during critical situations or crises. Any plan prepared by superiors, members of the crisis management team, and related employees to help the organization overcome a crisis in the best possible way is called a crisis management plan.

Why Crisis Management Plan?

? A crisis management plan helps employees to adopt a focused approach during emergency situations.

? The crisis management Plan elaborates on the actions to be taken by the management as well as the employees to save the organization's reputation and standing in the industry. It gives a detailed overview of the roles and responsibilities of employees during a crisis.

? Individuals representing the crisis management team formulate a crisis management plan to reduce the after-effects of crisis at the workplace.

? A crisis Management Plan helps the managers and superiors to take quick and relevant actions as per the situation.

? A crisis management plan protects an organization from inevitable threats and also makes it's future secure.

? Such plans reduce instability and uncertainty among the employees and help them concentrate on their work.

What is Crisis Communication?

Crisis Communication refers to a special wing that deals with the reputation of the individuals as well as the organization. Crisis communication is an initiative that aims at protecting the reputation of the organization and maintaining its public image. Various factors such as criminal attacks, government investigations, and media enquiry can tarnish the image of an organization. Crisis Communication specialists fight against several challenges which tend to harm the reputation and image of the organization.

Need for Crisis Communication

Crisis can have a negative effect on brand image. Crisis Communication experts are employed to save an organization's reputation against various threats and unwanted challenges. Brand identity is one of the most valuable assets of an organization. The main purpose of Crisis Communication team is to protect the brand identity and maintain the organization's firm standing within the industry. Crisis Communication specialists strive hard to overcome tough situations and help the organization come out of difficult situations in the best possible and quickest way.

Time Management

? Time Management refers to managing time effectively so that the right time is allocated to the right activity.

? Effective time management allows individuals to assign specific time slots to activities as per their importance.

? Time Management refers to making the best use of time as time is always limited

Features of Time Management includes:

i. Effective Planning

ii. Setting goals and objectives

iii. Setting deadlines

iv. Delegation of responsibilities

v. Prioritizing activities as per their importance

vi. Spending the right time on the right activity

9 798888 833919

Printed by Libri Plureos GmbH in Hamburg,
Germany